20 TOOLS FOR THE COLLABORATIVE CLASSROOM

Getting the Most from Your Partnerships

Rebecca A. Hines
University of Central Florida

Lisa A. Dieker
University of Central Florida

20 TOOLS FOR THE COLLABORATIVE CLASSROOM.
Copyright © 2014 by Rebecca A. Hines & Lisa A. Dieker

ISBN: 978-0-692-21639-2
Professional Learning Press

Books may be purchased in quantity and/or special sales by contacting the publisher, Professional Learning Press by email at info@collaborativepd.com.

Contents

20 Tools

As legislation shifts and shapes our educational practices and new buzz words come and go, two topics continue to be at the forefront in our field: Inclusion, and technology. While the focus of this book is inclusion, technology is highlighted as we consider strategies and tools to support all learners.

Over the course of this century, the inclusion of students with disabilities in general education settings has expanded in scope and expectation. The No Child Left Behind (NCLB) Act, initially authorized in 1965 as the Elementary and Secondary Education Act (ESEA), was signed into law on January 8, 2002 as a means of holding states, school districts, and schools more accountable for improving the academic performance of every student, including those with disabilities. The call for rigorous standards in the law has required states to hold annual assessments at specific grade levels and implement a comprehensive accountability system. With such a varied range of learners, however, implementing the policy has revealed the need for revisions of key components of NCLB. While the spirit of holding schools accountable for having high standards for students with exceptionalities remains, waivers have now been put in place and the legislation is currently being reauthorized under its original name- Elementary and Secondary Education Act. The Individuals with Disabilities Act is also slated for updates and reauthorization, although key points continue to be debated.

So what should we expect as more changes are on the horizon?

In an August 23, 2013 press release, the U.S. Department of Education stated:

The U.S. Department of Education has proposed regulations…to transition away from the so-called "2 percent rule," thus emphasizing the Department's commitment to holding all students to high standards that better prepare them for college and career. Under the existing regulations, States have been allowed to develop alternate assessments aligned to modified academic achievement standards (AA-MAAS) for some students with disabilities and use the results of those assessments for accountability purposes under Title I of the Elementary and Secondary Education Act and the Individuals with Disabilities Education Act. In making accountability determinations, States currently may count as proficient scores for up to 2 percent of students in the grades assessed using the alternate assessments based on modified academic achievement standards. http://www.ed.gov/news/press-releases

Under the Department's proposed regulation, students with disabilities will transition to college and career ready standards. New assessments are expected to better measure higher-order thinking skills and pushes critical and creative thinking back into the educational limelight. Rather than simply performing well on a multiple choice test, students will be expected to show that they can not only apply knowledge but generalize learning to other settings, communicate what they have learned, and solve complex problems.

How do we teach for this type of change?

This book includes tools for teachers that specifically address these areas of critical thinking and communication without abandoning our need to ensure students have mastered basic content. Ideas shared range from structures to make the most of the "tried and true" successful practices already happening in your classroom, to adding a new layer of assessment, technology, or instruction.

As we adopt new standards, whether common core or other, we must constantly focus on ensuring our curriculum is universally designed and accessible for all learners. States that have adopted the Common Core Standards require students with disabilities to learn targeted skills at targeted grade levels (especially in mathematics), so students having access to content at key points is critical. This book is designed as a planning guide to provide tools and resources that can be used across skill levels, grade levels, and content areas.

Before we get to the tools, let's review the basics.

Accommodations

While universal design for learning calls for us to add layers of representation, expression, and engagement to meet learner needs, we have long been using accommodations to support students. Whether it's to meet specific common core goals or other state goals, knowing basic accommodations is key for every teacher. To meet varied learner needs, try accommodations such as:

Highlight notes and text	Try using a livescribe.com pen, an erasable highlighter, or a tool such as Audio Note
Same skills at a lower level	Consider using a cross-age tutor to help create materials, a parent volunteer, or recorded presentation
Varying questioning techniques	Use Piaget's levels as a guide on the board and think about how to add a high and low level question about the same concept.
Small group tests	Why not use cooperative learning and let students complete tests both as a group and individually? Ultimately individual scores will stand, but this approach allows learners to build confidence and better understand academic success.
Change print and font size	Scan in or go to bookshare.org or projectgutenberg.org and get text that is already electronically available. Try a variety of font sizes, colors and prints to see what helps the student access text most easily.
Digital books	Learningally.com can provide electronic books for students with print disabilities (and numerous other sources).
Keep students informed of progress	Use classdojo.com or goalbook.com to provide students with feedback. We can also go "old school" with paper pencil or "new school" with daily short video messages.
Change response modes	Why does a student have to write or talk in front of peers? Before selecting one mode to validate learning, think about other options – producing a video, a cartoon, a drawing – the sky is the limit. A novel idea is to ask the student how he/she would like to show you what they know.

For the sake of this book, co-teaching will be generally defined as the practice of a general education teacher and a special education service provider (either a special education teacher or related service provider) working together to plan, instruct, and assess both students with and without disabilities in a shared setting.

Common co-teaching structures include the following:

Lead & Support. One teacher leads and the other offers assistance to individuals or small groups or carries out other managerial tasks.

Parallel Teaching. Both teachers teach same content, but each uses a different instructional method (one may lead hands-on, for example, while the other leads discussion-based). Both teachers cover same content and use same assessment, just use different strategies. Students choose preferred learning style.

Alternative Teaching. One teacher works with a small group or provides individual conferences while the other teacher works with the rest of the class.

Station Teaching. Teachers share responsibility for developing centers, and students rotate through activities. One teacher may lead a center to give specific feedback while other monitors other centers.

Team Teaching. Both teachers share the planning and instruction of students in a coordinated fashion.

Tip: No matter which structure you use, keep a shared clipboard on which you can take turns collecting data, checking papers, giving participation points, etc. while the other teacher is instructing.

Be sure you are passing the clipboard back and forth regularly for in-flight communication!

Two Service Delivery Approaches for Collaborative Settings

Co-Teaching

Two teachers share instruction, planning and assessing for a shared group of students with and without disabilities on a daily basis. This model provides the most direct support for the general education teacher as a special educator or other related specialist comes into the general education setting as a regularly scheduled part of the class.

Collaborative Consultation/Facilitated Support

This approach most often consists of a general educator and a special educator (or related specialists) collaborating primarily outside of class time. The general educator includes students with disabilities but actually co-teaches only part-time or not at all. The special educator provides support to students by regularly checking on IEP progress, course progress, and provides specific supports for the student to use in the general education setting. In some cases the special educator/specialist co-teaches a couple of days a week. This "ad hoc" approach is used in any number of ways and often varies school-to-school, district-to-district.

Collaborative Models and Layers We Can Add

Although this book will refer often to co-teaching, the simple fact is this: At its core, co-teaching is collaboration. Good collaboration starts with good communication and clarity in roles and expectation, whether formally co-teaching or using other models.

No matter which structure we are using, we can still meet the needs of diverse learners by rethinking our current classrooms. Use your partnership to add these new layers to your classroom. The goal is to be specific in determining roles, tools, and strategies. Each teacher brings *one specific* tool or strategy every day. Often, special educators have great learning and organizational strategies to share, for example. Bring them! Caution: Don't try to add multiple layers at once. Decide which one best fits your needs, and who will introduce it into your classroom. Introduce the strategy or structure, and give it time to take root. Meet two weeks later, and specifically ask yourselves: "Is this Working?" If yes, continue on and add another. If not, select a new tool or strategy, and repeat the reflective cycle.

Sample of Adding Specific Strategy: Cornell Note Taking

Teacher 1: "Today we are going to be continuing our work solving linear equations and inequalities. To begin, take out your notes from yesterday for a brief review. Make sure your notes are structured using the Cornell system. Look over your notes for 1 minute." Set timer.

Teacher 2 uses this time to take attendance, do a quick check for homework, or any other managerial items that occur daily and eat up instructional time.

Teacher 1: "Next, take one minute to write a summary from yesterday's notes." (after one minute):

"Are there questions from yesterday that were not answered? If not, let's prepare for today's notes, and listen as Mrs. Allen extends our thinking about linear equations and inequalities."

Teacher 2 begins content lesson.

Cornell Notes Structure

Questions / Keywords	Notes
Summary	

After content provided, **Teacher 1** instructs students to reflect on what they heard and write questions following the Cornell system.

http://lsc.cornell.edu/Sidebars/Study_Skills_Resources/cornellsystem.pdf.

Sample of Adding Specific Tool: PBL Checklist

Teacher 1 "I know we are doing the science project next week that includes a written component. I will create a checklist the students can use to ensure they are including all of the pieces to the assignment. PBL checklist has several areas of focus we could use. Which ones would you like to focus on for this activity? I will share a draft before copying it to be sure we are on the same page with the assignment expectations."

Teacher 2 "Sounds good. Here's the assessment I usually use. Let's focus on research and relating concepts as our area of emphasis- I don't think my usual quiz taps into those areas, so focusing on that will be great."

http://pblchecklist.4teachers.org/

Sample Layers to Add to the Collaborative Classroom

Co-teacher can bring new tools:	Co-teacher can bring specific strategies:
Rubistar	Note-Taking
Dragon Dictation	Writing
PBL Checklist	Reading
EdumotoVoki	Communication
Voicethread	Social skills
Slideboom	Behavior
Picture Dictionary	Participation
Virtual Manipulatives	Organization

Use your partnership to add specific layers based on the interest and teaching strength of each partner.

Now that we've considered the basics, let's get down to exploring 20 specific tools any of us can use to get the most from our partnerships.

What will YOU bring?

1. Co-Teaching Menu

If you are reading this book, chances are that you are already co-teaching, using a support facilitation model of some type, or are preparing to do so. Let's acknowledge from the start that previous reviews of co-teaching have found that teachers generally view co-teaching favorably, but research is limited. It's difficult enough to control for all of the variables in a single-teacher classroom when conducting research, so when another teacher is added things really get tricky. Considering that many districts, schools, and even teachers use the model in idiosyncratic ways, validating any one best practice can be problematic. So how can we be sure it works?

The best way to ensure that your co-teaching model is working is simple:

Use your partnership to add layers of instructional best practice to the classroom, and you will raise achievement!

In other words, it's not the model that makes the difference- it's the teachers.

At-a-Glance	Co-Teaching Menu
Who	Both teachers select roles from the planning menu.
What	One-page checklist of teaching roles and co-teaching structures for fast, specific planning.
When	Daily.
Where	Keep checklist handy for fast reference by either teacher, or to share with administrators if they are conducting walk-throughs.
How	Plan a specific time each week to review the menu and select roles for the following week. For example, we may decide we want to run oral assessments on Tuesday so we select the alternative co-teach model from the menu, and oral assessments. Wednesday we will run stations, so we look at the menu for ideas of which types to run.

To be successful, we must identify the layers we can add to our shared classroom, and decide who will "bring" what. Rather than thinking of co-teaching as a matter of "my turn, your turn", it should be "While you are…, I will…"

To gain clarity in roles and tasks, you might use the menu on the following page for planning. Better yet, use the concept to create you own menu specific to what each of you does well. Begin by first identifying which co-teach structure you will use on any given day (or structures), and find a corresponding role under the category. Decide which specific task you will be completing, and your partner does the same.

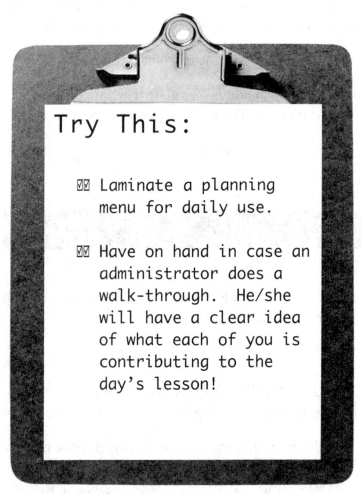

Try This:

☑ Laminate a planning menu for daily use.

☑ Have on hand in case an administrator does a walk-through. He/she will have a clear idea of what each of you is contributing to the day's lesson!

Co-Teach Structures

☐ **Station Teaching**
☐ **Alternative Co-Teaching**
☐ **Lead/Support**
☐ **Team Teaching**
☐ **Parallel Teaching**

Parallel Teaching

☐ Inquiry-based option
☐ Hands-on activity
☐ Project-based option
☐ Literature connection
☐ Direct instruction
☐ Skill-based instruction
☐ Other

_____
_____
_____
_____
-

Lesson Goal:

Station Teaching

☐ Discussion station
☐ Demonstration station
☐ Performance station
☐ Assessment station
☐ Writing station
☐ Independent practice station
☐ Skill review station
☐ Computer station
☐ Reflection station
☐ Reading station
☐ Extension station
☐ Other

_____

Alternative Teaching

☐ Writing conference
☐ Demonstration of mastery
☐ Oral assessment
☐ Goal setting
☐ Reflection on performance
☐ Coaching
☐ Other _____

Lead/ Support

☐ Content delivery
☐ Anticipatory set
☐ "Bellringer"
☐ Clarifying comments
☐ Learning strategies
☐ Observation data
☐ Concrete example/ demonstration
☐ Images/graphic support
☐ Note taking skills
☐ Coding behaviors

Team Teaching

☐ Selections from entire menu
☐ Added attention to:

_____
_____
_____
_____
_____
_____

Find a "formula" that fits!

Based on the co-teaching styles, what do you believe would be your preferred method of co-teaching?

Do you see yourself alternating roles, or finding one model that works best for you?

What specific tools can you bring to the collaborative setting?

What specific strategies can you bring?

2. Oral Assessments

By definition, knowledge acquisition involves complex cognitive processes: perception, learning, communication, association and reasoning. The term knowledge is also used to mean the confident understanding of a subject with the ability to use it for a specific purpose.

If we want students to truly understand skills and concepts, finding ways for them to show us or tell us is critical. Even if our goal is ultimately better test performance, students must be able to demonstrate that they have learned the material. Being able to communicate what they know is one way to ensure that they are undergoing a more

At-a-Glance	Verbal Response Checklist
Who	Either teacher. Sometimes one person or the other may be better suited to analyze the quality of the student response, but if there is a clear-cut answer or both teachers have shared content knowledge, either teacher is fine.
What	Quick tool for recording results of oral responses or demonstration.
When	Consider a regularly scheduled time of week to run through quick oral assessments. This makes it easier to plan. When you get the system down, you can often do a quick check of the whole class in as little as 20 minutes.
Where	Sometimes at student desk with one teacher checking an answer to a question that was on the board, or other times in a conferencing setting (two desks in back of room, table, wherever available).
How	Use the alternative teaching model with one person completing the assessment while the other person leads whole group. Allocate enough time to ask a question and wait for a response, but keep students to a time frame so individuals do not monopolize teacher time and all students have an opportunity. For example, one teacher may walk around with 10 words on a piece of paper and ask each student to point to an adjective.

complex cognitive process, and having the confidence to explain their knowledge is key.

Providing more opportunities for students to share their understanding through verbal communication provides a layer by which those who struggle with the written word can gain the confidence needed. Perhaps if we can encourage their confidence in expressing knowledge, in a verbal format, they will be able to later communicate it in writing when needed.

Using a form such as the **Verbal Response and Demonstration Checklist** is one way to keep track of mastery. The co-taught setting provides a perfect format in which to use such assessments, as one person can attend to whole class issues while the other performs the assessment.

Sample Verbal Response Checklist to Track Mastery

	Date: 3/12/14 Concept: *Matter*		Date: Concept:		Date: Concept:	
	Demonstrated Mastery?		Demonstrated Mastery?		Demonstrated Mastery?	
Student	Yes	No	Yes	No	Yes	No
Ricky	X					
Tanisha	X					
Mandi		X				
Ramon	X					

Providing more opportunities for students to share their understanding and demonstrate mastery through verbal communication provides a layer by which those who struggle with the written word can gain the confidence needed. Perhaps if we can encourage their confidence in expressing knowledge in a verbal format, they will be able to later communicate it in writing when needed. Alternative teaching allows optimal opportunities for oral assessments, goal setting, and much more. EITHER teacher can have brief one-on-one conferences with students while the other manages the whole-class activity!

For example, you might use the alternative teaching model with one person running an oral assessment while the other leads a whole-class lesson. Use an assessment checklist to document results. Allocate enough time to ask a question and wait for a response, but keep students to a time frame so individuals do not monopolize teacher time and all students have an opportunity.

Sample Questions for Quick Oral Assessment

Concept: Matter

1. Tell me what matter means in your own words.
2. Tell me one example of matter in this room.
3. Give me one example of matter at your home.

Remember to keep it to 1-2 minutes

Planning for Oral Assessments

Adding verbal assessments simply takes committing to day/time for conducting the assessments, identifying which teacher will lead the assessment, and a structure for conducting the assessment. Begin planning discussions with questions such as:

1. What is one key concept we are teaching right now?
2. What are two things every student should be able to tell us about this concept?
3. When could we use Alternative co-teaching for one of us to do an oral assessment?
4. Which one of us will print the Verbal Response Checklist to use for the assessment (or create our own)?

Finding a consistent pattern for these types of assessments can make it easier to manage. If we know we don't have much shared planning time, we can commit to Wednesdays as our oral assessment day, for example, so we know we are using alternative teaching that day. Planning means simply identifying the single skill we want each student to know and applying our structured oral assessment system.

Verbal Response & Demonstration Checklist

	Date: Concept:		Date: Concept:		Date: Concept:	
	Demonstrated Mastery?		Demonstrated Mastery?		Demonstrated Mastery?	
Student	Yes	No	Yes	No	Yes	No

3. Audio Notes

When it comes to adding layers of universal design for learning (UDL) to our classrooms, the tools available are endless. One easy layer to add to support students with special needs and to increase opportunities for all students is audio responses. Whether used as a layer of UDL so students can respond orally or as a note-taking support, computers, iPads, iPod Touches, and even cell phones can be used to accomplish this goal.

One simple online tool for those of us who don't have mobile devices readily available in the classroom but do have an Internet connection is Vocaroo, an online voice recording service. When it comes to simplicity, it doesn't get much easier than using Vocaroo. It's simply click, and record. The tool is designed for easy use, and is basic enough for even young learners and those with limited technology skills. After you have recorded, the recording is posted online and a web link is automatically generated. Send the link to anyone, and he/she can play the recording.

At-a-Glance	Audio Notes
Who	Either teacher decides to take lead on this tool.
What	Students to take notes orally.
When	Daily.
Where	On handheld devices, classroom computer, wherever arranged by teacher leading the use of this tool.
How	Several options available. Either: - Student record notes after listening to a lecture or discussion. - Student records lecture - Teacher records brief note summary and posts online

Simple Ideas for Audio Tools

1. Students read and play back passages from books to increase fluency
2. Students record a short reading sample and e-mail to parents or grandparents
3. Students submit responses to content questions and e-mail to teacher
4. Students record "think aloud" to explain work
5. Students record notes after listening to a lecture or discussion
6. Students with verbal difficulties record audio messages to exchange with audio "penpal" to practice enunciation
7. Students with language difficulties work on increasing word production through oral language
8. Students work on writing skills by reading their own writing passages aloud and listening to playback to check for clarity

Of course, the opportunities are limited only by your imagination as a teacher. Need more ideas?

Perhaps students prepare a brief verbal summary after a lecture and mail it to themselves for later review. Even younger students might practice this idea of remembering three key points they hear, and restating in their own words. Putting it in writing can come later, but at least the skill will be introduced.

A tool like Vocaroo (vocaroo.com) can be used to support this type of reflection and note taking. This free tool is one of the simplest free tools available, with no sign up required (It should be noted, it's in the "beta" stages, so it's hard to tell how long it will be available for free). The best plan would be to use this simple, free tool to explore the potential of oral assessments. It's tough to find an easier tool than Vocaroo to get started with audio options!

How about older students who struggle with note taking and studying?

Try any of the note-taking features on most cell phones these days, and be sure students know how to use the features on their own devices. While most have a notes feature, there are inexpensive apps such as Audio Note that provide even more options. With a teacher's permission, a student could be recording the lecture in the classroom while adding his/her own written notes on the device. Drawing tools and the ability to use images are included, so a student can take notes visually while still capturing the lecture. Audio note is available as a free app, or can be upgraded for a small price. Both versions allow users to record audio, write text, dictate over images, and highlight key points. The upgrade allows the notes to be sent, however, while the free version does not.

Whether used as a way for students to interact differently with material, reflect on learning, or enhance study skills, student- generated audio through tools such as Vocaroo and Audio Note, it is increasingly easy to add an audio option for every learner.

Who on our team will explore audio options?

How might we introduce this to our students?

Will we share the idea with all students, or just those with IEPs?

4. Note-Taking with Feeling

Traditional note taking is still a skill valued by many, but what about students who have physical disabilities and can't write easily? Or those whose brain and hands just don't connect to allow them to put on a piece paper what appears easy for many classmates? In some cases, these students cease to learn the minute they are asked to take notes.

If you are of the "tough love" era and believe "they must take notes to learn", remember: Just as a student in a wheelchair might want to walk, a student with dysgraphia (a writing disability) may want to write. Neurologically, however, the student may not be any more capable of writing than a student with a physical disability. Beyond the issues faced by those with specific disabilities, we have to also remember that many students are just not very good at taking notes, and that some don't really "know" what is important.

At-a-Glance	Note Taking with Feeling
Who	One teacher delivers content, other teacher introduces and models use of the strategy.
What	Note taking strategy that appeals to affective part of the brain.
When	Daily, or whenever notes are expected.
Where	Any classroom.
How	Often used with lead/support co-teach structure. One teacher writes notes on the board, support teacher draws circles and triangles around key points as described in this text.

Despite all of these potential challenges, we can provide a simple tool that may make note taking less painful for some students. The best part is, this simple strategy can benefit your entire class. So using the procedures provided, think about how you would go about creating a co-taught class that happily takes notes in a way that is successful for everyone.

As notes are given you are at the board and you circle words with blue that are important to really think about and emotionally respond to – war, fear, fighting, etc. Then you put red triangles around words that you know will be on the exam.

Adding Support

The teacher modeling the strategy invites students to copy her/his notes and strategy. Students with mild writing disabilities, or others who need supports, can be given a page with circle and triangles on it and be expected to write in those two areas the words that have been marked on the board. Once completed, they can trade those notes for full notes (which you will have previously prepared)

Students with more severe disabilities in note taking may only try to write what is in the triangle and they can put words or images or just check the boxes. If they do so, then they get a copy of the notes. The basic idea is to encourage students to hone in on what is most important in a class lecture or discussion.

Why note-taking?

20 minutes after learning something, you've forgotten 47% of what you learned

Check out more interesting facts about note taking in an infographic at

http://www.coursehero.com/blog/2011/10/19/infographic-write-it-down/.

Supported Notes

Use supported notes for students who can take key words (circle) and what is critical to know for the upcoming assessment (triangle) but are unable to fully capture class notes. Students trade these in for copies of full notes.

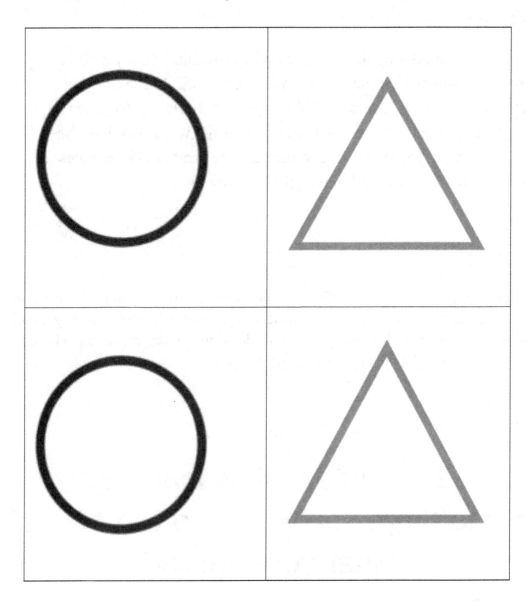

5. Penny Jar

High tech tools are great for so many reasons, but sometimes it's nice to go "old school" to deal with behavior and motivation. Try this simple but effective approach for coaching students as a group into mastering both social and academic goals.

Start with approximately 50 pennies and two glass jars. Put the pennies in one jar and put a + sign on it. Put a – (negative sign) on the other jar.

Write three things on the board with an eye and an ear and tell everyone what each behavior you are expecting from them looks like and sounds like.

At-a-Glance		Penny Jar
Who	Either/both teacher. Maybe rotate days so they see that both of you are working to shape behavior, and both simultaneously add to the jar.	
What	Positive behavioral support using token system.	
When	Daily to start, then fade as needed. Bring back from time to time just to keep them on their toes.	
Where	Any classroom, any population of students.	
How	1. Decide who will be kicking off the Penny Jar approach, and pick a day to start.	
	2. Designated person brings in jar and pennies, and presents brief overview to students of how it will work.	
	3. One or both teachers contribute to the jar throughout the class period.	
	4. Remember to reflect with your partner at the end of the week on how it is working, and tweak as needed.	

When they are doing the three things you want them to do, leave the jars alone. If they are not doing a behavior you expect, don't say a word. Just noisily start dropping pennies from the "+" jar into the other "-" jar. If, at the end of the day, they have more in the positive than the negative they can cut their homework in half or some other "free" random reward – don't tell them in advance.   Let each day be a surprise.

This simple intervention really is about awareness raising. Behavior becomes habitual in our classrooms, so this is a gentle reminder to everyone. When several days of positives add up, you can tell them that you will randomly reward them over 2-3 days. Even high school kids are a sucker for this idea, and starting with something cheap like Smarties candies to get their attention is a light, easy reminder to think about our actions in the classroom.

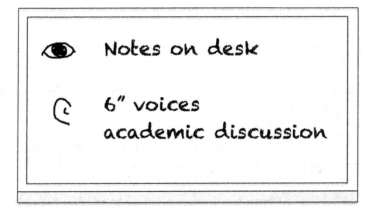

Getting Started: Penny Jar Planning

1. You may start by having a daily penny goal that students reach each day.

2. Try using 4 jars as teams compete to have the most pennies left in the jar. In this model one teacher could be the leader for one team and the co-teacher could be the leader of the other.

3. Determine:

Who will take care of the jars?

What will be the reward?

Who will give out the reward?

What will we do if a student does not respond to the group?

Will any student need his/her own individualized jar?

6. Flipped Classroom

Ready to move to a more project-based classroom? Consider the flipped classroom concept. The premise is simple: Students view key content in recorded video format before coming to class, so in-class activities are application based. High school chemistry teachers Jonathan Bergmann and Aaron Sams are most often credited with the concept, which they designed as a way to maximize instructional time, review and reinforce lessons, and allow more individualized instructional interactions with students in class.

On its website, the Flipped Learning Network notes that there is a difference between flipped learning and a flipped classroom. Flipped learning is defined as

> "..a pedagogical approach in which direct **instruction moves from a group learning space to the individual space**, and the resulting group learning space is transformed into a dynamic, interactive learning environment where the educator guides students as they **apply concepts and engage creatively** in the subject matter." *flippedlearning*.org

	At-a-Glance	Flipped Classroom
Who	Either/both teacher. One teacher could create the recorded content and assign the way to access the information for homework while the other creates the higher-level activity that will occur in class.	
What	Recorded content for students to access outside class that you expect to be mastered prior to coming to class (typically basic knowledge or key concepts).	
When	Viewing the recorded basic content is assigned as homework. Students who did not view or need remediation might view or review upon arrival. Students do not advance to the hands-on application until they have mastered the prerequisite content from recordings.	
Where	For any classroom, any population of students. Many teachers do their actual recordings using the camera built into a laptop, phone, iPad, or a webcam.	
How	Typically the flipped concept is assigned to be viewed during	

homework time and the application is assessed and happens at the next class period. Videos can be posted using Google Docs, YouTube, or any school designated site.

Four Pillars of Flipped Learning

F   **Flexible learning** modes and environment in which students choose where to learn.

L   **Learning culture** changes to learner-centered, with class time used for exploring content at greater depths with more personal relevance.

I   **Intentional content** is the focus as educators find ways to help students develop conceptual understanding and procedural fluency.

P   **Professional educator** remains the central ingredient for effective learning, through design, delivery, feedback, assessment, and reflection.

http://flippedlearning.org/

Flipping It: Out with the Old and in with the New

	Old	New
Lesson Objective	Students will learn the names of and identify the stages of mitosis in book and on worksheet	Students view recording and come ready to name and show the stage of mitosis. Show evidence as they enter the classroom; Classify stages of mitosis on slides in the class
Lesson Objective	Students will understand the concept of main idea of a story	Students will come to class ready to share main idea and rewrite story from their perspective in collaborative groups. Each group picks one character

Flipped Classroom Planning

First determine where you will house the videos. Review free options such as Google Docs and YouTube as possible storage. Creating a **YouTube** channel may be easier than you think, and a transcript is automatically generated. You can record right into YouTube from your webcam, or upload from your computer. Edit the transcript to ensure accuracy, and closed captioning is ready for optimal accessibility. You can set privacy features as needed if you are worried about security. Google Docs provides another easy-to-use option and offers the bonus of storing other file types as well.

Concept	Who will Record?	Application activity

7. Parent Contact

When it comes to keeping parents informed, make sure you have a set pattern. Our favorite is a "good cop/bad cop" described below. Dividing roles in the classroom adds a layer of clarity and ensures we remember to touch base regularly.

Also, don't forget to send home some type of letter at the beginning of the year introducing both of you as the teachers in the classroom. We suggest using a simple letter, unless you already have a full set of "digital" parents who prefer other forms of communication. You of course will want to tailor your letter depending on whether you teach elementary or secondary level students.

We also suggest that, when co-teaching, both names are listed on the report cards that go home, on any letter you send, and most importantly on any concern or celebration note you send home. Collaborating teachers should be seen as a team, not only in the eyes of the students but also in the eyes of the parents.

At-a-Glance	Good Cop/Bad Cop
Who	Both teachers. Finding a pattern for rotating the parent contact works well: One week you write the e-mail/newsletter, the next week I do- but we BOTH sign it!
What	Consistent and frequent parent contact.
When	Weekly, or preferably daily if we have a system such as a class Edmodo or blog.
Where	Every classroom.
How	Post online, print hard copies, or send via e-mail. Preferably parents select which format works best for them, and we make it available both digitally and in hard copy.
	Take your lesson plan book and each week determine one teacher as a "good cop" and the other "bad cop". The good cop is expected to make at least three phone calls home that week to celebrate a students success (ideally include a student who last week got a bad phone call home). The bad cop for that

week then will be the person who has to write up any student, deal with any discipline referral and of course call parents. Changing up this routine makes it so that students are never sure why both of you are calling and provides a balanced approach.

Sample Statement for Collaborative Setting Introductory Letter

Dear Parents,

We are excited to be working with your child in our xx grade classroom this year. As co-teachers, we are both committed to the success of each and every child in the classroom. You will be receiving communication from both of us as we work together to help your child have a successful year. We are excited to work with you, your child and each other to make this a great year.

Our basic expectations in our class include:

1. Courtesy and consideration for fellow students and teachers

2. Prompt response to directions

3. Consistent effort and work completion

You should have received the full code of conduct for the school, and the syllabus for our class. Please let us know if you have questions about the information provided, and it will be our pleasure to help you get the most of this school year.

Sincerely,

Becky Hines and Lisa Dieker

Looking for new ways to reach parents? Try using Edmodo (a tool like Facebook but a close social network), Goal Book (a way to communicate around IEP goals), or simply create a Google Drive for ongoing communication with parents and to share class files.

Screen Shot from Edmodo

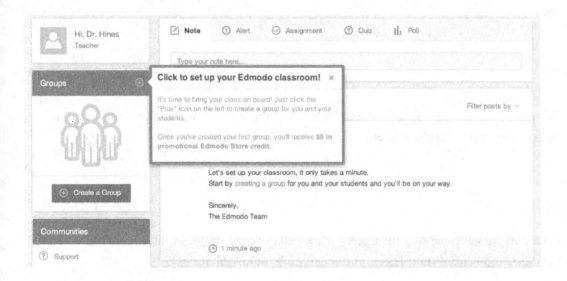

Google has now created its own program, Google Classroom, to help keep teachers, learners, and parents connected. This new tool, launching in beta preview in 2014, is designed to help teachers make, collect and track student assignments, and to help them better communicate with their classes.

The Classroom app is a streamlined version of similar tools that already exist, designed to simplify the workload for teachers. The program incorporates its Docs, Drive and Gmail programs to make assignment creation and tracking easier than doing these things manually. For those of us using Google products, familiarity with the existing programs might make this a good choice for getting started with digital connections.

Reflecting on our Parent/Family Communication

Are parents aware of our school policy on inclusion?

Are we expecting any questions or concerns from parents regarding changes to our school's inclusive practices? If so, what will we tell them?

If co-teaching, how will we explain the role of the special educator or support teacher?

What will we tell parents of students with disabilities who worry their child is not getting enough individual attention or support?

How can we keep parents informed of everyday happenings so they feel connected to the class and school (and less apprehensive about any changes)?

8. Online Games and Quizzes

If you have a teaching partner, let's not forget to use both of you to the maximum. Instead of thinking about both of your roles as equal presentation time, it might be time to begin planning around specific roles. For example, every Tuesday my job might be to find and/or create the best online quizzes or games to reinforce the big idea for the week, and present to the class. In contrast, my co-teacher would be leading and developing the lesson for the day.

Problem: Not enough time to create new online material

Solution: Offer opportunity for students to do this as homework, extra credit, or service

At-a-Glance	Online Games & Quizzes
Who	Either teacher can design and create. Perhaps one teacher writes or gathers the questions, while the other agrees to create the online activity.
What	Unlimited opportunities for students to practice and receive immediate feedback using online games & quizzes.
When	Create review games/quizzes weekly, and build a cumulative review system so students can practice in March those same concepts learned in October. Share the information with students, and encourage them to review on their own time, as homework, or in any creative way you and your partner envision.
Where	Post online on your own class website, or create an account within a program such as: ☑ Quizlet ☑ Study Stack

How	1. Determine key concepts taught each week- what do you want ALL students to know?
	2. Determine who will gather questions and who creates.
	3. Use one of the tools above to create a review quiz.
	4. Show students how to access the activity, and consider giving credit for those who access outside of class.
	Many programs allow students to turn a single quiz into a variety of review activities, all with the click of the mouse.

Keep in mind there are hundreds of online resources, but finding time to locate them seems to be the frustration for many of us. We suggest that making this a role of one of the co-teachers (or, again, switching each week) is a great way to enrich what is going on in your classroom.

Tools for Creating Quizzes & Games

Quizlet is a free tool allows you to create your own online study tools, and with the click of the mouse convert them to games and quizzes. It even has a feature that allows the questions to be read aloud under the "Learn" tab.   quizlet.com/

Brainpop includes digital content in the form of short animated video mini-lessons. Quizzes are included, as well as other content materials. Purchase required. www.brainpop.com

Quia allows users to create online quizzes, games, activities, surveys, web pages, and more. Like Quizlet and other tools listed here, it also has a large database of activities already created by others that anyone can use. Skip the registration and click on the Shared activities section to browse by topic or textbook title and find material already created and ready for use.

Kubbu is an e-learning tool designed to facilitate teachers' work and enhance the learning process, and includes a tool for sharing with groups and analyzing results. www.kubbu.com/ .

You can also go to Lisa Dieker's delicious site for a variety of other sites for teaching and learning: www.delicious.com/ldieker

9. Formative Assessments

Imagine this: As one teacher is teaching, the other can constantly be assessing everything from homework to social skills to engagement. That's how we raise achievement in a collaborative classroom!

Planning for this type of routine is simple. Just determine which days and times we will designate as the "Quick Check", and make it a routine. Tuesdays and Thursdays at 10 a.m. are Quick Checks, for example.

First question is: Which days and times work best?

Next question is: Which one of us will do it this week?

And, finally: Which formats will we use to assess this week?

	At-a-Glance	Assessment Checklist
Who	Either/both teachers. You might try rotating "assessment expert" weekly.	
What	Routine for ensuring students are making satisfactory progress.	
When	Weekly.	
Where	Anywhere.	
How	Set aside time to note progress on content and social skill development. The content objective will likely be the same for all students in the classroom, and only some will have specific social goals. Complete the form weekly and place somewhere for easy access so either teacher can review as needed for parent or student conferences.	
	Also, **look for trends**. If all students are passive, maybe we need to add new layers to our instruction!	

Make sure that both teachers are clear not just on the objective, but also on the exact evidence or outcome you want students to produce. For example, the objective from the state standard today might be "The student understands that all matter has observable, measurable properties." That is great to state, but what evidence will students show?

Co-teachers might decide that they want each student to be able to either name, write or show an observable, measureable property of two items (a measuring cup and a book). Now both teachers know that throughout the lesson everything they do should lead to students being able to define and give examples.

One teacher can decide what the performance measure will be to show the objective, and the other can find a way to gather the data. Perhaps during the closing activity the special education teacher is moving around the room asking each student to give one observable and measurable property of each item and noting it on a checklist (see Verbal Assessment, Tool 2 in this book). Or, perhaps the closing activity is that in groups each student must add one more way to observe and one more to measure and their answers are recorded. Either way, this is basic data-driven instruction and can be that simple. It's essential to great teaching- and great co-teaching.

---

4 Easy-to-Implement Formative Assessments

1. Exit slip for students to write one concept learned in class.

2. Greeting students at the door the next day and asking them to state a concept or key point as they walk into the room.

> One concept I remember from today is that two sets have the same cardinality if they can be put into one-to-one correspondence

3. Student self-rating (1-5) of understanding from previous day.

4. Having each student, as homework, find one thing in his/her house related to topic.

Use the information gathered through these formative assessments as data for instructional decision making. It seems that so often teachers see data-driven instruction as a standardized or formal test, but if daily you find ways to assess your instructional goal then you don't have to wait four weeks for a test to tell you who is and who is not learning your content.

Three additional points to remember about assessment in inclusive settings:

1. Fair does not mean same or not equal.
2. Both teachers need an understanding of modifications & accommodations on assessments for students with IEPs.
3. We must keep appropriately high expectations & standards for ALL students.

Consider this: Can one of us become the Assessment Expert for the team, and focus on having very specific, varied formative assessments daily? Can we better track the results to help us focus on problem areas?

Planning for Formative Assessments

1. How are we assessing now?

2. Are we regularly assessing social and behavior goals?

2. What are three other ways we can assess on a daily basis?

3. Which way will we try first?

Tip: Use an Assessment Checklist to make sure each student is meeting your content and social goals for the classroom.

Assessment Checklist

Student	Content Objective Met	Social Skill Objective Met	Homework Objective Met	Engaged (E) Passive (P)

10. Learning Stations

Promoting the idea of communication and problem solving is best accomplished in teams, but managing group environments can often pose a challenge- especially for those students who are not accustomed to self-management.

If you have two teachers – why not have 2 groups, 4 groups, or even 6? If one teacher can handle 3 small groups in a class then 2 could handle 6.

Barriers to station teaching? The noise, the noise, and the noise! The following are ideas to help think through grouping in cooperative groups and stations.

One Location and Direction

If you have a room the size of a shoebox, remember to use the corners. Also, you can always have short stations that include one group standing instead of sitting or even sitting on the floor.

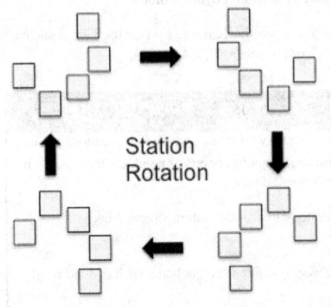

Station Rotation

So let's say you have groups in "U" shapes in each of 4 corners. One group could be a listening center (no noise involved there) and the other could be working on an independent task.

If co-teaching, each teacher has one group to lead in discussion, direct instruction, etc. Now, instead of 1:25 or 1:30 teacher/student ratio, we have 1:5 and students receive specific teacher instruction and feedback with groups changing every 15 minutes. For longer blocks of times – let's say 30 minutes- you could use this model over 2 days. Either way, you have several important skills going on at the same time.

We also suggest you revisit the concept of "true" cooperative learning. We often hear teachers say that they cannot put students into groups because they won't learn anything or someone else will do their work. Revisit the concept of jigsaw cooperative grouping and be certain to have students access the social skills of peers.

When you use the core principles of cooperative learning (positive interdependence, promotive interaction, individual accountability, group processing) immediately your high flyers should fly and your students who struggle should begin making progress toward success in groups. One partner might become the cooperative learning "expert" to ensure this strong research-based strategy is a tool in your toolbox.

Refresh your memory on principles of cooperative learning by viewing videos such as the one found at http://www.youtube.com/watch?v=HEh8Z0sbiRE

Station Teaching

Which would you prefer to lead?

Discussion station
Demonstration station
Performance station
Skill review station
Computer station
Reflection station
Reading station
Extension station
Other:
Review Game station

At-a-Glance	Cooperative Learning
Who	Both teachers. One may circulate and answer questions while the other awards participation points or conducts individual oral assessments at student desks.
What	Cooperative strategy to promote interaction and deepen processing.
When	Daily, hourly, weekly – the more the better (if it is done well!).
Where	Any classroom.
How	Remember, cooperative learning is NOT group work! Be certain to assign roles and hold students to high levels of accountability.

Using complex tests in your classroom? Try using the Jigsaw strategy to aid your students, especially those who are struggling readers. Check out this video for an example of Jigsaw being used in a classroom that meets the Common Core State Standards: https://www.teachingchannel.org/videos/jigsaw-method

How does it "look" in the classroom? Use a basic instruction sheet such as the one below designed for a middle level science classroom:

Teamwork Instructions

You will work as a team to complete science labs. All participants should discuss each question on the lab sheet. When you are finished, turn in one paper for the group in the Completed Lab bin. Each person on your team will write a response to the Think About It question in his or her own science notebook.

Before you begin, decide who will be in each of these roles:

- **Lead Investigator** – Reads the introduction and the procedures and makes sure all instructions are followed .
- **Recorder**- Writes down the group's responses to lab discussion questions.
- **Materials Manager** – Makes sure materials are ready and acts as coach and timekeeper.

Getting Started:

1. The lead investigator will read Science in the Bag to introduce the lab.
2. The materials manager will make sure all materials are ready.
3. The lead investigator will read the first step of the procedure. All students will work together to carry out the step.
4. The lead investigator will ask everyone to discuss the first question.
5. The recorder will write down the group's answer.
6. The materials manager will measure and prepare supplies.
7. Use this pattern to complete each step on the lab sheet.
8. Recorder makes sure all team member names are on the lab sheet.
9. Lead investigator makes sure everyone has written answer to Think About It in his or her science notebooks.
10. Materials manager makes sure all materials are placed neatly back in place.

- ☑ Learning stations don't have to be fancy- just thought provoking!
- ☑ Avoid thinking of station teaching as "group work". It's not the same!
- ☑ Use one teacher-led discussion station for station-teach situations with co-teacher.

Try using a learning game to structure an independent station while teachers work at others. Students are accustomed to following rules in game play, so it provides an automatic management system and structure. Use a tool such as Tools for Educator's Board Game Maker found at **http://www.toolsforeducators.com/boardgames/** to create your own custom review game board. Write clear instructions for the game, and students will more easily manage an independent learning station.

Sample Custom Game Board

As an example, we created the Co-Teach Review Game on the following page. Using the board game maker website, we first created a custom game board. There are templates on the site to design a basic game, but writing instructions and coming up with questions is the job of the creator. We used the option of "create board game with images and text". Using this option, we chose the images we wanted, and added game text. The instructions we had to invent separately, so the the ones on the following page are what we came up with. Something basic such as this works well.

Be as creative as you wish with instructions and questions. You can use flashcards, questions from homework- anything you would like students to review and discuss. The goal is to promote independence on the part of the learners, and the game implies a framework familiar to many students.

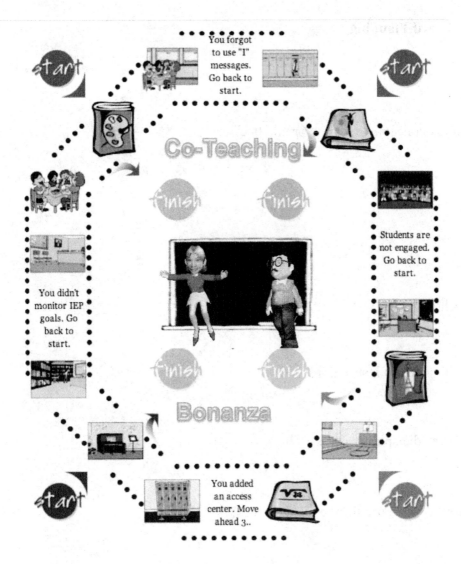

Directions: Roll the die. Answer the question that corresponds with the number shown. If your group approves your response, move ahead the number shown on the die. The first player safely to finish is the winner!

If you roll a:

1   Name a co-teach structure
2   Name one new tool you could add to your classroom
3   Find out one new thing about the person on your left
4   Name a type of data you could collect in your collaborative classroom
5   Name one consideration for co-planning
6   Describe one new type of assessment you could add in your class

Game Board Planning

What is our objective?

Key words/concepts to review or practice:

Who will make up rules?

Who will make up instructions?

Will we use die/spinner/cards?

What text will we use for the blank spaces?

Who will create the game board?

Who will print (and laminate)?

When will we try it?

11. Pretests

Just as we need ongoing assessment to ensure that students master a concept, we also want to make sure our students are not bored. If students have mastered a concept before you begin teaching it, don't waste their instructional time listening to topics they already know. Extend thinking through customization.

> **Textbook publishers** offer some of the easiest opportunities for us to pretest and extend/review learning. If you are using texts, check out the publisher site for resources. It's worth a look!
>
> Co-teaching? One teacher might mine the offerings on your textbook publisher's website or in the teacher's edition of the text to find a simple, specific way to customize.

Differentiate teaching roles by one teacher taking a lead in assessment from beginning to end of a unit. One teacher becomes the person who charts out an enhanced assessment process, beginning with creating a pretest and following through with daily and cumulative assessments. The lead assessment teacher analyzes pretests to differentiate instruction for a unit (why make kids do the same thing if they demonstrate mastery beforehand?) and designs new formative and summative assessments. The goal is to prepare to differentiate from the start of a lesson or unit based on specific student skills and needs. Using the principles of UDL, stay away from a single paper/pencil pretest. While you can include this as a part of your pretest, you might be assessing what a student cannot do (read) instead of what he or she knows about your topic.

We recommend including some simple techniques such as the following for your pretests:

1. Using a video recording device, ask each student to come to the back of the room and talk for 1-2 minutes about his/her knowledge of the upcoming topic.

2. Have students create a semantic map of as many ideas as they know of before you start a unit. Ask them to add to their map daily, weekly throughout the unit with a different color – now you have a pre and post assessment.

3. Ask students to draw an image with as much detail as possible about the topic.

4. Give students 20 quiz questions but be willing to read and write responses (or have a student talk responses into the flip camera) for all involved.

If co-teaching, remember there are two teachers so use both of you to do oral summaries, group analysis or whatever works in getting to what students know before you start. The oral assessments using the alternative co-teach model as earlier discussed in this book are an example of a structure well-suited for this type of pretest. After all, behavior and boredom often go hand in hand. Once you pre-assess use a model such as station teaching or alternative teaching to provide enrichment or pre-teach to catch up those students with large gaps.

At-a-Glance		Pretests
Who	Either teacher takes lead.	
What	Brief assessment given prior to beginning a new topic.	
When	Regularly.	
Where	Every classroom.	
How	Develop a procedure, and stick with it! Use pretests from the text when available to save time. One teacher administers and grades the pretest, and shares results with co-teacher. Both teachers determine how to extend the learning for those who have already mastered a concept before it is taught, and how to provide access to review materials to students far below the norm of the class.	

College & career readiness?

Have students practice the ACT, GED, or SAT with pretests at sites such as http://www.freetestprep.com/. Weaving brief, non-graded opportunities for students to practice with materials such as these can instill confidence or reveal weaknesses so students are not surprised when it's time for the real thing.

12. Vocabulary Review

May we say, BORING!! How do you make such a critical task sizzle?

If co-teaching, remember you have two people – which one of you is creative? Whoever it is, take the lead in this task. If it is neither of you, then ask students to come up with some exciting ways to review vocabulary. If you are collaborating using other models, find a creative colleague who can help you brainstorm. Here are not only some great ideas, but also some pitfalls you want to stay away from.

First of all, remember to keep it simple. We realize the reading book or social studies book might give you 20 vocabulary words, but they don't always tell you how to chunk the information. Do you remember 20 names of students from a foreign country after just one week? The brain is really meant to learn about 7-10 things at a time. We suggest that you expose the class to all 20, but commit 7 to long-term memory. Some students will remember all 20, while others only remember the 7. That may be 7 more than the student would have otherwise learned, while the higher achievers will remember the 20 either way.

At-a-Glance	Vocabulary Review Routine
Who	Either teacher takes lead. Often this is a good, specific role the special educator or specialist can take to contribute to content when not much shared planning time is available.
What	Specific, focused approach to reviewing core content vocabulary.
When	Daily, 5-15 minutes per period.
Where	Every classroom.
How	Determine who will take lead as vocabulary expert. Research methods for teaching vocabulary. Choose best option for your classroom, and implement. Be sure to check later test scores for the class to determine whether the focus is paying off with improved performance.

How do we accomplish this? Try these 3 tips:

1. Have students draw images of the words.

2. Draw words randomly from a hat daily, and have volunteers act out the words. Remember no more than 7 in a day!

3. Plan, plan, plan. Use a chart like the one below to line out your weekly vocabulary schedule. Determine a lead teacher in your partnership who will be in charge of vocabulary for the unit. That person focuses on *specific* ways to teach, and follows up consistently with mastery activities.

	Key Words	Strategy for Teaching	Mastery Check
Mon.			
Tues.			
Wed.			
Thurs.			
Fri.			

In the case of vocabulary instruction, less really is more. We have had co-teaching teams across the country tell us when they moved to the essential big idea and 7 key vocabulary words something magical happens – all students succeed.

Need a more formal product? Publishers such as Pearson offer full vocabulary products to help support learning. If you have students who are failing because they struggle with the basics, it may be time to explore this type of option at your grade level. For an example, check out the Pearson site at http://www.pearsonschool.com and search for *Vocabulary Their Way*. Sample lessons are included.

You might also go to https://www.youtube.com/watch?v=L_6dHOc46FE to hear *Vocabulary Integration in the Common Core*, a podcast by literacy experts Dr. Donald Bear and Dr. Shane Templeton. They discuss how to incorporate vocabulary strategies into the school day to meet common core standards. For a more full exploration of the topic and video, check out the We are Teachers website (http://www.weareteachers.com), and look in the lesson area. Search "vocabulary" for more information on the topic.

No matter which resources or strategies you use, developing a system and being consistent matters most. Once the system is designed and roles agreed upon, try any of the strategies here or do a simple web search of your own. Just remember to keep it simple!

13. Graphic Organizers

Yes, this may seem like old news and perhaps you are already using some form of graphic organizers (visual tools that show relationships between facts, terms, or ideas within a learning task, sometimes referred to as concept maps, story maps, and advance organizers). But even if you are already using these tools, re-examining or adding more graphics and graphic organizers is a great way to differentiate your roles and is a concept strongly supported by research for all students. It may be time to spruce up the ones we are using, or create new visual materials to support our key concepts.

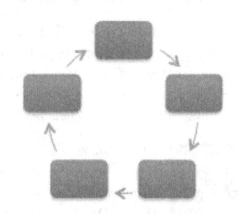

At-a-Glance	Graphic Organizers
Who	Either teacher takes lead.
What	Visual means of organizing information.
When	Daily.
Where	All courses.
How	Use tools such as Smart Art in MS Word, materials from textbook publishers, or any of the many free online tools to find or create a custom graphic organizer. Be sure to teach students to create their own as well!

Consider whether you want to use a linear, a cyclical or a hierarchical graphic organizer. These can easily be printed from Smart Art using Microsoft Word. Never tried using Smart Art? Simply open MS Word or PowerPoint, and go to Insert/Smart Art Graphic. Or, click the icon on the main screen. You will instantly have images to show hierarchy, relationships, processes, lists, and more. Teach students to use this tool or other templates to create their own high-quality organizers.

Sample Smart Art Images

Students can be supported through the use of graphic organizers that use vocabulary words and concepts to organize and identify key concepts that need to be included within their science explanations, research papers, or other activities.

We often like to use this idea with station teaching.

One station is to create the organizer, the other is to edit and the third is to enter "no man's or woman's land" where they are simply writing a short paper or paragraph from their graphic organizer.

In the first two stations anyone can help another but in the 3rd station they can only get support from the two teachers who can be editing and shaping students writing.
Try this as a weekly activity or an end-of-unit activity to make it fluent, systematic, and purposeful.

Try This: Give students a blank organizer sample created with Smart Art in Microsoft Word prior to a class discussion. Ask them to complete it using information from the lesson. Take a moment at the end of the lesson for students to compare notes with other students to see how they used the graphic organizer.

For students with disabilities who need support, get them started with a key term in each box so they have an idea how to proceed. Share one completed by the teacher after students have discussed so they can be certain they included key details.

You might also use images such as these for visual text organizers, which we all should be preparing prior to the introduction of new material. Make a habit of using visual organizers for the textbook.

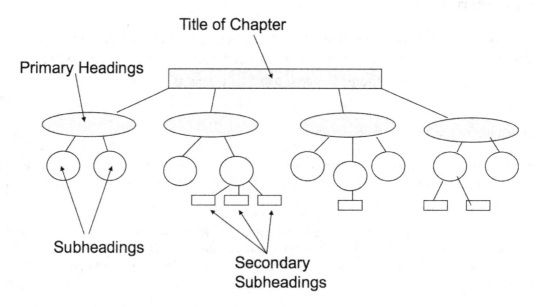

Thinking about organizers:

How could you use these?

When could you use these?

Who will prepare our visual organizers?

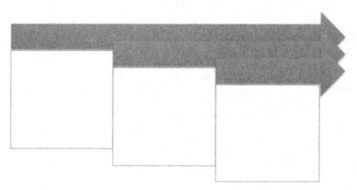

Of course there are tons of online resources to also help you create good graphic organizers. **Check out edhelper.com's selection, or Education Place's graphic organizers.**

14. Class Dojo

Of the overwhelming number of tools and apps being utilized by teachers in schools everywhere these days, Class Dojo is one used across grade levels and class types. On its website, the developers describe Class Dojo as a "classroom tool that helps teachers improve behavior in their classrooms quickly and easily. It also captures and generates data on behavior that teachers can share with parents and administrators". All true, but this free tool in the hands of the savvy special educator has the potential for many other uses as well.

Backed by what they describe as "Silicon Valley's top investors", the company boasts that it has grown faster than any education technology company in history. According to an article on the Tech Crunch website, developers Sam Chaudhary and Liam Don identified the biggest problems teachers face in the classroom every day by interviewing several hundred educators, and managing student behavior rose to the top of the list. In response to this information, Class Dojo was launched in August 2011 to help teachers control unruly classrooms.

The system as designed is based on basic behaviorism: rewards and consequences. Teachers assign students an avatar and award points or consequences from their laptop, tablet or smartphone. The program allows teachers to track data over the course of days or across time, and even has a feature for sharing results with parents.

At-a-Glance	Class Dojo
Who	Either teacher researches the tool and creates a class.
What	Free online behavior management system that allows you to easily keep points using your computer or smart phone.
When	Daily.
Where	Every classroom, across classrooms if used to support specific students with IEP goals.
How	1. After reading this section, determine how it will be used. 2. Decide who will create class.

3. Populate class.

4. Customize goals in Class Dojo.

5. Show colleague how to use it!

6. Download to phone or tablet so you are not tethered to a computer.

7. Track behaviors.

8. Use parent contact feature and other elements as needed.

Class Dojo can run on an interactive whiteboard, a computer connected to a projector, or even just a smartphone, tablet or iPod touch! The only thing you really need is some kind of computer device in the classroom (just one, for the teacher, is enough) and an Internet connection.

Using the program is simple and intuitive, and can be used creatively to move beyond a simple behavior management plan.

Three ways to support students with disabilities using Class Dojo

1. Monitor classroom participation

Participation is one of the default goals on the program, and using this systematically and awarding students credit for class participation could not be simpler when using this tool. For example, one high school co-teaching team in East Liverpool Ohio used the tool to get 100 percent participation during class discussions. While one teacher lead the discussion, the other noted who responded to questions. When a student had his point, he was not allowed to respond again. Everyone knew the goal was 100 percent, so they encouraged non-participators to respond in class.

Another creative participation use? Why not drop in on students participating in cooperative learning assignments and award participation for those who are actively contributing to the team. Although you may already have a system for assessing the activity, awarding participation credit in short intervals is a good way to help those learners who have not traditionally been successful see that they can earn credit for engaged time. And remember- let the points count toward their grade! Incremental credit is helpful for getting kids back on track after years of experiencing academic failure and defeat.

2. Oral Assessments

Instead of waiting until student perform poorly on written tests, let's ask them to demonstrate mastery every day. Using Class Dojo, a teacher could do quick oral assessments and keep track of performance with ease.

Identified noun   **Identified verb**

Because the program is customizable, teachers can write their own goals rather than using the behavior goals that are already on the tool. Instead of writing only behavior goals, consider academic goals as well and get in the habit of asking students to perform daily. It can be as simple as asking a student to point to a noun in a sentence, and then to a verb and tapping your iPhone to record the data. A chart can be printed with results at any time.

3. Monitor IEP Goals

Because you can create any number of "classes", create one for your students with IEPs. Customize the behaviors with very specific instructional and behavioral goals from the IEP, and check in on students each day. Record progress, and you have a dated running record of students' progress!

Whether you are using Class Dojo as a behavior management tool or for more creative purposes, you can get started using the program quickly and easily. The intuitive interface is easy to navigate, and most basic questions you might have are answered on the Help link.

You will need to sign up for an account before using the app, but the app allows you to award points from your cell phone or iPod touch as you circulate the classroom. The site can be up on the screen for students to see, on the Smartboard, or information can be kept private.

Planning for Class Dojo

What goals will we set?

      Behaviors to create/monitor:

      Academic goals to create/monitor:

Could we use this for group activities or oral assessments?

Who will set up the classes online?

Who will take the lead in monitoring progress?

When will we start?

15. Modified Literature Circles

No matter the content area, we can use literacy activities to tie learning to real-world applications and support a differentiated inclusive environment. Vocabulary, discussed in Tool 12, is an example of a literacy skill that can be used across settings. If co-teaching, the special educator or other support teacher could bring this to every content area. Literature circles, or a modified version of these, provide another option for promoting literacy.

Consider a math class, for example, working on fractions. Three different readings could be selected from current magazines or journals. One teacher states:

> "Today we will be reviewing fractions. To begin, let's take a look at some readings to situate our thinking.

At-a-Glance	Modified Literature Circles
Who	Both teachers participate. Each finds reading for at least one circle.
What	Student-led discussions of readings.
When	Daily, weekly depending on content area.
Where	Although most often used in reading/language arts, can be used across content areas.
How	1. Find reading materials that tie to the content (if not language arts class).
	2. Assign groups or allow students to choose topic of interest.
	3. Assign meeting dates.
	4. Assign roles.
	5. Act as facilitator for discussions.

If you'd like to think about fractions in cooking, circle up over here to read this article and recipe. If you'd like to frame the content around construction, take a look at this article and blueprint. Anyone who would like to think about this through engineering, take a look at this journal article..."

In Literature Circles, students are assigned various roles to cover reading material to be read in or outside of class. To use this strategy, share the following role descriptions with students:

Literature Circles Role Descriptions

In this activity the roles are as follows:

Question/discussion – The student who leads the discussion and questions the group as they read.

Clarifier – The student who clarifies any misunderstandings with the group and also the only student who can ask the teacher questions about the assignment.

Summarizer – The student who summarizes what was read for the group.

Predictor – The student who will predict what will happen next in the reading.

Artist – Can be doodling and drawing the entire time. The student is to provide an artistic rendition of what has been covered to this point in the story and the image can change or be redrawn each time.

These roles can be changed and adapted to fit the needs of your learners. Other roles can be added based upon the needs of the students and the student's strengths (the actor, the storyboard creator, the Lego or wiki stix representation creator). Just keep in mind that typically groups of 4-5 are best as too many students make each literature circle too long to complete. Students can go through the literature circle in as little as 2 minutes and can be student-directed reading or teacher-directed reading and discussion.

Planning for Literature Circles

Which of us will take the lead on this?

How often will we use literature circles?

Will we give credit? How?

	Goal	Reading Selections
Monday		
Tuesday		
Wednesday		
Thursday		
Friday		

16. Conferencing

Are your first graders, middle schoolers or high schoolers really going to be ready for college and/or the workforce? Isn't that the goal of school?

Consider some of the following ideas to ensure all students know how to set and reach goals, and students know how to talk about their abilities and disabilities. The alternative co-teach model is perfect for this approach, and it's just a matter of deciding on any given day whether the special educator or general educator will coach students in these skills. Rather than a long whole group lesson on topics like goal setting, this approach increases one-on-one interactions between students and teachers, allowing for a truly customized learning experience.

At-a-Glance	Conferencing
Who	Either teacher leads.
What	One-on-one focused discussion with individual students, with focus on increasing self-advocacy.
When	Weekly. For students with IEPs, be sure to hold meeting at beginning of year and also near IEP meeting time.
Where	Can be done as group activity, then moved to individual discussions in designated area of the room.
How	Consider using "tap back" method. Call first student back to conference, have discussion (approximately 2 minutes, unless discussing IEPs or preparing for IEP meeting). When completed, ask student to "tap" a classmate back by lightly tapping shoulder. If the student has already had a conference, he/she simply shakes his head and another student is selected. This non-verbal way of calling students back reduces the distraction of a teacher calling out names while the other is teaching.

Conducting Coaching Conferences

These activities may begin with a whole-group activity such as goal setting, with students then rotating through conferences for feedback from a teacher. The amount of time for conferences might vary, but in an inclusive classroom you will want to rotate every student through a conference whether or not he/she has an IEP. General education students rotating through conferences can be asked a different set of questions or coached in their own specific areas of need. These students may not need as much time in the conference, but they deserve to have a teacher's undivided attention in coaching them toward academic success.

Goal Setting

Student	Goal		Goal Check Up	
	Date		Date	Met goal? Comments
1.				Y/N
2.				Y/N
3.				Y/N
4.				Y/N
5.				Y/N
6.				Y/N
7.				Y/N
8.				Y/N
9.				Y/N
10.				Y/N

Students should set all goals. Recommended check-up period should be no later than two weeks from date goals are set.

Considerations for Students with Disabilities

Students with disabilities might use extra time in the conference, and be asked to create summaries, letters or presentations to help others and themselves better understand their disability and their needs. Ideally, this takes place typically at the beginning of the year and again near the time of an IEP meeting. Students at elementary level can create a written piece or video to help others understand their strengths and weaknesses.

Middle school students might create a Power Point, Prezi or video to share their ideas and high school students should write letters and make a plan to talk with their teachers. Being able to seek support is a critical skill for college and career readiness!

Use a guide such as this to focus these discussions or projects.

Self-Advocate Planning Guide

	Materials for IEP meeting	Strengths	Areas of Focus	Disability (in my words)	Other things to know about me...
Elementary	Book Comic Video				
Middle School (attends IEP mtg)	PowerPoint Prezi Audio/video				
High School (attends and leads IEP meeting)	Formal letter to teachers Verbal discussion				

Looking for a way to teach your students about proper etiquette when it comes to discussing disabilities?

Check out these lesson plans from the Museum of disABILITY History:

Trading Cards Lesson Plan

Understanding Etiquette Lesson Plan

For more lesson plans and to explore the museum virtually, go to
http://museumofdisability.org/educational-resources/

Planning for Conferencing

1. What are the greatest current needs of our students:

   - ☑ Self-advocacy
   - ☑ Goal setting
   - ☑ Communication
   - ☑ Other:

2. Who will lead first conferences?

3. When we will start?

17. Tech Planning Guide

Whether you have one computer in your classroom, multiple devices, or a BYOD (bring your own device) policy, technology is firmly rooted as a part of contemporary classrooms. Some schools are putting iPads in the hands of every learner, while other educators remain skeptical about the use of these devices as an instructional tool.

 Research on the effectiveness of specific apps and tools is scarce to date, but articles in the popular media including the New York Times, Boston Globe, ABC News, and other sources are reporting on the use of these tools in the classroom, making these practices more a part of contemporary classroom culture.

No matter what technology you have, any available devices can likely be maximized to provide students with increased access to content and increased access to rehearsal and review. To put these tools to best use in today's classroom without risking the integrity of the learning event calls for us to consider how to maximize the tool using best practices of teaching in general. In many classrooms technology use is often unstructured, and may lead to increased motivation but leaves teachers wondering, "Is this working"?

At-a-Glance	Tech Planning Guide
Who	Either teacher creates. Teacher or students complete the form.
What	Systematic way to structure and assess technology-based activities.
When	Whenever students are using devices as independent learning tools.
Where	Classroom, computer labs.
How	Use a planning tool such as the one below. For every app or program used, identify the purpose. Once identified, ask yourself this: How will we assess what they have learned today using this device?

If the devices are being used for creating, researching, video editing, etc., then answering the "Is this working" question rests with the teacher. Keeping pre/post data on student engagement, speed to engagement, project completion, time on task, etc. can help reveal whether the tool is helping meet classroom and individual goals. For those of us using specific apps that are more game-based, consider adding a layer of structure that calls for students to be more purposeful in their use of the tool.

Purposeful teaching and learning involves goal setting, organization, clarity, structure, adaptive practices, and evaluation. Consider how we might apply these steps to becoming more "purposeful" with iPad and device use, such as:

Planning. Rather than jumping from app to app or game to game, students design a plan for apps they will use during the time they are on the iPad or computer. For young learners or students with communication difficulties, this may be a picture schedule (picture of the app or icon) or other planning method. The key is to encourage students to plan for their learning, and stick to the plan.

Goal setting. Have students play designated games, and record their best score. Ask them to set a goal for the score they would like to achieve by the end of the week (or other time frame).

Progress monitoring. Use graphs and journals to document progress. On each occasion in which students are playing educational games, have them plot their score for specific games played before switching to a new app. If the app is not game-based, consider having them write a quick note in a journal describing progress made (or not made). Periodically check in with students to discuss their charts and journals.

If there are not enough devices for all students, using a simple schedule so every student can rotate through activities in a station-style setting is the solution. Include specific expectations that are clear and be sure the activity is well designed. You might even video the instructions and leave them open on the computer so students hear a teacher's explanation or reminder of the rules. Unsupervised open access to the computer is not the objective here.

Technology Planning Guide

App	Goal	Activity	Assessment
			Checklist Log Game score Chart Other:
			Checklist Log Game score Chart Other:
			Checklist Log Game score Chart Other:
			Checklist Log Game score Chart Other:
			Checklist Log Game score Chart Other:

18. Access Center

In the past, accessibility in the classroom has revolved largely around students with disabilities. As Universal Design for Learning has become a part of the vocabulary of education, however, the scope has been broadened. It is now expected that all teachers give multiple ways for students to take in and engage with course content. Add increasingly available technologies that support productivity for everyone, and keeping up with the changes seems daunting. How can we do it all?

In the new Common Core standards, technology plays a prominent role in every discipline and at every grade level for all students. For students with disabilities, access to and fluency with technology is particularly critical. In schools across the country, students with print disabilities are accessing, analyzing, and comprehending grade level texts using hand-held, mainstream text readers. Students with fine motor or executive functioning disabilities are composing essays on par with their non-disabled peers using mainstream text-to-speech software. Making these tools a regular part of the classroom continues to be a challenge for many educators.

At-a-Glance	Access Center
Who	Special education teacher might take lead if he/she has specific tools. Either teacher can lead.
What	Specifically identified area in the room where students go to access information or supports.
When	Whenever needed.
Where	Wherever you can find space to put it.
How	1. Identify a spot in the classroom to place the access station.

2. Both teachers brainstorm which types of supports to include, and which instructional material to add.
3. Determine which teacher will take lead on setting up the station.
4. Determine who will lead a brief mini-lesson with the class to introduce tools and rules of the center.
5. Consider tools from elsewhere in this book to include as resources to put on your access station!
6. Establish routine for updating center materials.

Creating and labeling a space in every classroom specifically designated as an ACCESS CENTER is a place to start. Whether we are working in co-taught, consultation, or self-contained settings, ALL students should understand that

Access applies to everyone.

As with all planning in our classrooms, we begin with the end in mind. What do I want my students to have access to that they do not currently have? What individual needs exist for students with low incidence disabilities? What behavioral needs might be addressed with a fresh approach? What types of extension opportunities are available for my highest achievers?

Steps to Starting an Access Center

1. Choose location

2. Organize available hardware (computer, headphones, etc)

3. Locate digital resources to include:

    ☑ Review Tools
    ☑ Research Tools
    ☑ Production Tools
    ☑ Support Devices & Tools
    ☑ Extension Tools

4. Locate Non-Digital Items such as:

- ☑☑ Practice workbooks
- ☑☑ Extra reading materials
- ☑☑ Activities with written instructions (crafts, for example)
- ☑☑ Brain teasers
- ☑☑ Relaxation supports

5. Post instructions

6. Present "mini lesson" to introduce to students

7. Add new materials

8. Steer kids to finding appropriate levels of challenge/support

Tip: Be purposeful in your design, and consider changing featured websites to match the standards you are teaching.

Example: If students are working on continents, you might put Fact Monster as your featured website. But rather than having kids go to the main website, load it in advance to the page on continents!

There are many commercial products for computer-based learning today, but free activities abound on the web that can help get you started with independent access centers. We suggest that, as a way to use consistent language for the Access Station, you might categorize tools or activities in the following ways:

Productivity Tools

Encouraging students today to see themselves as producers rather than consumers begins with, well, telling them! Check out the Student Interactives under Classroom Resources at www.readwritethink.org to promote productivity. Simple sites like these might be featured for a week with the expectation that all students will find time to create a specific product. Rather than waiting for a laptop cart to become available and doing the activity as a whole group, students might be expected and encouraged to find time during the school day when they have completed work and can get to the access center to complete the simple activity. For those students who need support, schedule a specific time to ensure they complete the activity. Besides the language arts element, the goal is independence and teaching students to manage time!

Review Tools

Most major textbook publishers today have companion Web sites for their textbooks, sometimes at no additional cost. Finding the textbook Web site and showing students how to access it gives them unlimited opportunities to extend or review content in exactly the same language and style they are learning using your classroom materials.

As earlier discussed, Quizlet is a free flash cards and study games Web site. The site is easy to navigate, and students can choose between reviewing flashcards, games or tests on subjects already in the database or added by any user. For the student who is difficult to keep on task for an entire class period, consider a few minutes of review/practice in the Access Center to break up the period. Have the site preloaded or bookmarked, and set a timer. A quick break may be just what is needed to keep a student engaged. The learner chooses the type of activity or test delivered, and responses are scored automatically.

Support Tools

Even though we may use this area with all students, ensuring that specific tools to support specific learners are available is critical.

ReadPlease2003 is a free download that allows users to have text read aloud from any PC. Of course, there are any number of screen readers available, so choose the one that works best for you and your students. IPads and other tablets have these features built in, so be sure to check the Accessibility options in Settings.

Dragon Dictation is a must-have, and is a free app on mobile devices.

Goal setting worksheets as discussed earlier offer a different approach. If students need to create goals for themselves, either during a crisis or to plan for instruction, the access center is a great place to take a moment and get started. When all students use this center, it is not stigmatizing when a students uses the space to accomplish a specific support task.

Tip: Make sure students know how to locate these tools for themselves!

The bottom line is, all students should understand that in the classroom learning never ends. If you finish one activity, everyone needs access to more. Creating a space that promotes this idea- and provides access for students who need specific supports-begins with a few simple changes to our classroom environment.

The simplest way to get started is to first look at what is already available on the computer or device itself. Forget the Internet for a minute, and just look at the device. If it's a PC, go to Start/Programs and look for the folder called Accessories. Look in the Accessories folder for the title, Accessibility. Computers were built to be accessible, and this is where you can find the tools to use with specific types of learners.

In the accessibility area, there are settings that can be adjusted to accommodate specific disabilities. In some cases, there is even a step-by-step question series that will help to customize the computer just by answering key questions. For students with visual impairment, size of the screen can be adjusted. For students with physical disabilities, "Sticky Keys" can be checked so that keystrokes aren't repeated when a person cannot remove a finger from the keyboard quickly. Explore, and you will find tools that may be useful for specific students with whom you are working.

Apple offers a wide range of features that are ready to go with a tap of the device.

Remember: Access doesn't just mean assistive tools for persons with physical disabilities. It can mean access to computer-based review materials for everyone, access to instructions, access to extension activities, therapeutic "cool-down" activities for students with behavior issues, etc. This area can be about creating a space for meeting individual learner needs, in whatever way needed.

Teach ALL students in the inclusive setting to use and be aware of the accessibility features on the computer. This way, if someone with a visual impairment sets features to accommodate him/herself, the next person who uses the station can set them back to the original settings if needed. You never know which of your students may have a family member at home who could use these features, too!

19. Comics

As teachers look for ways to engage students and use principles of universal design for learning while still meeting standards, sorting through digital tools can be time-consuming and overwhelming. One website that offers ease-of-use, sample lessons, AND ideas specific to students with disabilities is Make Beliefs Comix, where students can make their own comic strip in minutes. Besides the fun visuals for students, the site offers lots of resources and ideas for teachers as they add a layer of UDL to any classroom.

Creator Bill Zimmerman and site illustrator Tom Bloom both share a background in

At-a-Glance		Comics
Who	One teacher learns the tool and introduces to students when confident.	
What	Free online comic creator.	
When	Use as an assessment option whenever possible.	
Where	Classroom, computer lab, homework.	
How	One teacher takes the lead and learns the program. Present mini-lesson to class. Be brief! Students interested in using the tool will pick it up quickly.	
	Use it as an option for students: "You can either write a paragraph explaining the conflict in the story, or create a four frame comic that communicates the conflict. Be creative, and ready to explain your thinking!"	

journalism, and bring their talents to educators through the site.

"My intent is that you will regard this site as a safe place where you feel empowered to create and to test new ideas and ways to communicate through art and writing," states Zimmerman on his site. He offers 21 ways to use Make Beliefs Comix in the classroom, which includes specific suggestions for educators for everything from academic tasks such as practicing new vocabulary and introducing creative writing to practicing conversation skills and social skill training. Scroll to the bottom of the page and you will also find a link to a section entitled SPECIAL NEEDS. In this area, you will find ideas from teachers of students with special needs who share strategies for varying types of learners.

Getting Started

Unlike many sites, there is no sign-up procedure necessary for giving it a try. Log into the site, and begin creating! Note of caution: The site is very much designed for contemporary users, so don't expect a lot of written directions for getting started. Creating is intuitive on the site, but some users may feel more comfortable clicking the red Getting Started button near the top for written instruction. There is also a Menu Help button under the menu to the left, so check there for help navigating actions.

Need for a way to get started without jumping into the creating mode? Teachers can begin introducing more graphics and visuals, or add a layer of differentiation using one of the **PRINTABLES** available free on the site. Simply click the tab on the website, and you will find student-friendly pages you can print for students that include the same characters they will see when they create their own comics. The printables cover a wide range of academic organizers, as well as specific pages for students with autism, second language learners, social/emotional activities, and more.

Another layer is provided through a **DIGITAL WRIT-ABLES** section. This section allows students to write directly on the screen on a single cartoon. A writing prompt is provided, with the intent of encouraging students to begin putting words on a page.

In addition to the web-based tools, creators just released an iPad app for 2014 . Whether you're a comfortable computer user who can easily navigate the comic creation feature or a fledgling willing to add a new layer, Make Beliefs Comix has something for everyone.

Planning for Comic Creation

1. Who will check out Make Beliefs Comix or locate other resources?

2. How could we use this?

    ☑☑ Assessment tool for an upcoming activity?
    ☑☑ One of us makes comics to stress key content points?
    ☑☑ Other ideas?

3. When will we try it?

4. How will we assess?

Created using Make Beliefs Comix

Graphics in this section from http://www.MakeBeliefsComix.com. Used by permission of author and creator Bill Zimmerman.

20. Reflection

Every time we step into a collaborative classroom, or any classroom for that matter, cues are read and decisions must be made. What's going on here? Who is working? Can I do something that will change the climate in here right now?

Teachers tend to be good at reading cues in the classroom, and understand when things are going well or not going well. The problem is that often when we read a cue and see that something is not working, we do not feel we have an alternative that we can shift to immediately to change the current condition.

How many times have we seen students not engaged, or not listening? We see this, and subconsciously ask ourselves, "Is this acceptable?" The problem is, even when we feel it isn't acceptable another question arises: "Do I have alternatives available?"

At-a-Glance	Reflective Decision Making Model
Who	Any collaborating teachers. Ask a friend to observe you if you want an objective view of your partnership.
What	Structured reflecting on our co-teaching practices.
When	Weekly to start. Try to get into a routine in which you plan to reflect- maybe on Friday afternoons. What worked for the week? What can you try differently next week?
Where	Wherever you like to meet or plan.
How	Print the Reflective Decision Making Model and place it on a clipboard. As you are co-teaching, consider the questions in the chart. Use the responses from this flowchart to guide a discussion about things that are currently working, and things you might want to change. If roles of the teacher or student engagement are problems, look for solutions throughout this handbook.

We often don't have a "Plan B" to revert to in-flight, so we keep exhibiting the same teaching behavior and generating the same responses from our audience.

This book is about ensuring every teacher has a "Plan B" at the ready, and proposes that the special educator can also be the change agent in collaborative settings to break this cycle. Consider the following decision making model to prepare for each co-taught setting.

Co-Teaching Reflective Decision Making Model

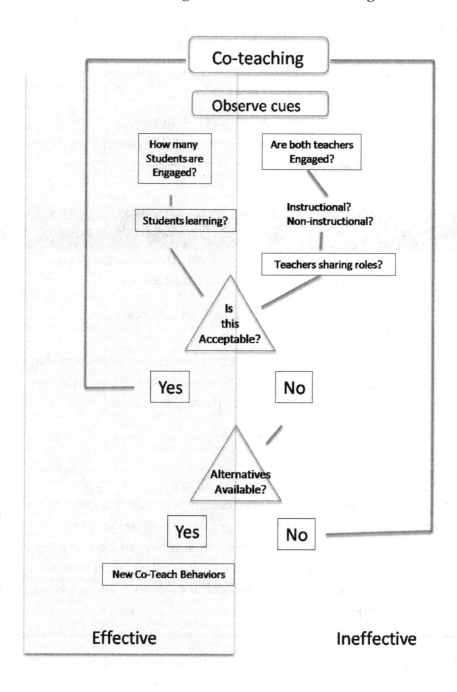

The following discussion points can also be used to lead your reflective conversations and plan for the future.

Considering Success of our Partnership

Plan time to reflect on the following questions regularly, possibly at the end of each unit or marking period.

About what percentage of students are currently engaged during our daily lesson?

If an outsider were observing our classroom, she/he would see:

The best part of our co-teaching partnership at this point is:

As we look for more layers to our partnership, the part I would like to focus on first is:

Ready for More?

When you feel you are up to it, video tape yourself co-teaching on a "typical" day. With your co-teacher, play back random portions of the class period and notice how it looks objectively. Are all students engaged? Are we both satisfied with the progress of the class on this day?

Use specific language to discuss what you notice that seems to be "working", and things that you may wish to improve upon. Also include language to describe how you are feeling at different times during the lesson.

Ultimately, remember a simple fact: Success breeds success. Once you have found one tool that feels comfortable and useful in your partnership, it will be easier to add more. Choose one tool from this book, the one you feel will be easiest to implement and most needed by your students, and give it a try. Implement it systematically, and give it time to succeed. Set a date, approximately two weeks out, to reflect on whether or not it worked for you and your partner.

First tool we will try:

Date we will begin using the tool:

Date we will reflect on success:

If the first tool you try doesn't work, drop it and pick up a new one. If it's too early to tell, keep going with it and set a new date to reflect. If the tool you added worked, keep it and add another! Continuing to **add new layers is the key** to success for our students, and to success in our teaching partnerships.

Visit http://www.collaborativepd.com/20-tools-printables.html for printable copies of the tools mentioned in this book.

CPSIA information can be obtained
at www.ICGtesting.com
Printed in the USA
FSOW04n2000071217
42184FS

9 780692 216392